MAR 0 3 2018

WORLD WAR I

BATTLES
OF WORLD WAR I

BY
JOHN HAMILTON

Maxim Machine Gun

Abdo & Daughters
An imprint of Abdo Publishing | abdopublishing.com

abdopublishing.com

Published by Abdo Publishing, a division of ABDO, PO Box 398166, Minneapolis, Minnesota 55439. Copyright © 2018 by Abdo Consulting Group, Inc. International copyrights reserved in all countries. No part of this book may be reproduced in any form without written permission from the publisher. Abdo & Daughters™ is a trademark and logo of Abdo Publishing.

Printed in the United States of America, North Mankato, Minnesota.
112017
012018

Editor: Sue Hamilton
Graphic Design: Sue Hamilton
Cover Design: Candice Keimig and Pakou Moua
Cover Photo: Getty
Interior Images: Alamy-pgs 14, 24, 40 & 41; Getty-pgs 8, 9, 11, 15, 23 & 30; Granger-pgs 4-5, 20-21, 26, 27, 28-29, 32, 34, 36-37, 38 & 43; Illustrated London News-pg 13; iStock-pgs 1 & 3; John Hamilton-maps-pgs 6, 10, 17, 21, 25, 29, 33 & 39; National Archives-pg 31; National Portrait Gallery United Kingdom-pg 35; The Image Works-pgs 7, 12, 19 & 42; Wikimedia-pgs 16-17.

Publisher's Cataloging-in-Publication Data

Names: Hamilton, John, author.
Title: Battles of World War I / by John Hamilton.
Description: Minneapolis, Minnesota : Abdo Publishing, 2018. | Series: World War I | Includes online resources and index.
Identifiers: LCCN 2017946704 | ISBN 9781532112867 (lib.bdg.) | ISBN 9781532150722 (ebook)
Subjects: LCSH: World War (1914-1918)--Juvenile literature. | Military campaigns--Juvenile literature. | Battles--Juvenile literature.
Classification: DDC 940.4--dc23
LC record available at https://lccn.loc.gov/2017946704

CONTENTS

The Guns of August 4
Battle of the Marne 8
    Marshal Joseph Joffre 11
    The Christmas Truce of 1914 13
Tannenberg and Masurian Lakes 14
    General Paul von Hindenburg 19
Gallipoli 20
Verdun 22
    General Henri Philippe Pétain 27
The Battle of Jutland 28
Slaughter of the Somme 30
    Sir Douglas Haig 35
The Third Battle of Ypres 36
The World at War 40
The Desert War 42
    Thomas Edward Lawrence 43
Timeline 44
Glossary 46
Online Resources 47
Index 48

THE GUNS OF AUGUST

"The First World War killed fewer victims than the Second World War, destroyed fewer buildings, and uprooted millions instead of tens of millions—but in many ways it left even deeper scars both on the mind and on the map of Europe. The Old World never recovered from the shock...."
—Edmond Taylor, *The Fossil Monarchies*

In 1914, the clouds of war loomed on the horizon. Europe had not seen a large-scale conflict in more than 100 years, since the time of Napoleon. The misery of war seemed like a distant memory. Late that summer, millions of young men polished their weapons and put on colorful uniforms.

Trouble in the Balkan region of southern Europe pitted nation against nation. Complex alliances between the most powerful countries of the world led to mistrust. Diplomacy failed. The Central Powers of Germany, Austria-Hungary, and the Ottoman Empire (present-day Turkey) squared off against the Allies, which included France, Russia, and Great Britain. Many other countries were eventually dragged into World War I, including the United States.

In August 1914, Scottish Guardsmen march out of the depot at the Tower of London on their way to war.

National honor was at stake, and war seemed unstoppable. Most people welcomed it. Eager soldiers on both sides believed a great adventure was about to begin. They were sure they would all be home soon. Within a few short weeks, however, people realized that this war would be unlike any other.

The generals thought their war plans would result in quick victory. They hoped their armies could sweep across the battlefield in mass attacks. That strategy had worked well in previous wars.

But the plans went disastrously wrong. New weapons proved more lethal than anyone imagined. Rapid-firing rifles, machine guns, and improved artillery made it easier to defend territory. Attackers rushing forward in the open were slaughtered.

There would be no quick way to win. Attackers could not deliver a blow that would end the war with one swift strike. Instead, the armies were stuck in a quagmire. They were doomed to a war that would last four years and kill millions of people.

The battles of World War I were the bloodiest the world had ever seen. Writers of the time struggled to describe the battlefields. They used words like "meat grinder" and "killing fields." People couldn't believe what was happening. Generals who weren't used to fighting with modern weapons sent men by the millions to die in needless attacks. That is one of the most tragic parts of the war. So many men died for so little reason.

In August 1914, the stage was set. Like a runaway locomotive careening downhill, the fighting began, and there was nothing anyone could do to stop it. The following pages look at the major battles of World War I, leading to the Russian Revolution and America's declaration of war in 1917.

Canadian troops face an onslaught of German soldiers at Ypres, Belgium.

BATTLE OF THE MARNE

September 5–12, 1914

"You will be home before the leaves have fallen from the trees."
—Kaiser Wilhelm II, Germany

The First Battle of the Marne was a major turning point early in World War I. It marked the end of Germany's rapid invasion of France. Shortly after the battle, the German "war of movement" became bogged down in a years-long period of trench warfare.

Germany had always feared fighting a war on two fronts, against enemies on two borders. Germany knew it would be almost impossible to win a war fighting France in the west and Russia in the east. To overcome this problem, German military planners developed the Schlieffen Plan. Named after Field Marshal Alfred von Schlieffen, it called for German forces to invade France and quickly knock it out of the war. Germany could then turn its full attention to defeating the massive Russian army to the east.

Excited German troops head for the Western Front unaware of the horrors that await them.

French troops make a stand, trying to drive back German forces. Thousands of French soldiers were killed defending their homeland.

In early August 1914, German forces swept through Belgium. They did this to bypass heavy French defenses along the German-French border. After crushing the tiny Belgian army (and executing hundreds of innocent civilians), German troops swooped southward into France and began capturing territory. This period of fighting is often called the Battle of the Frontiers. Tens of thousands of French soldiers were killed. It seemed that France would fall to Germany.

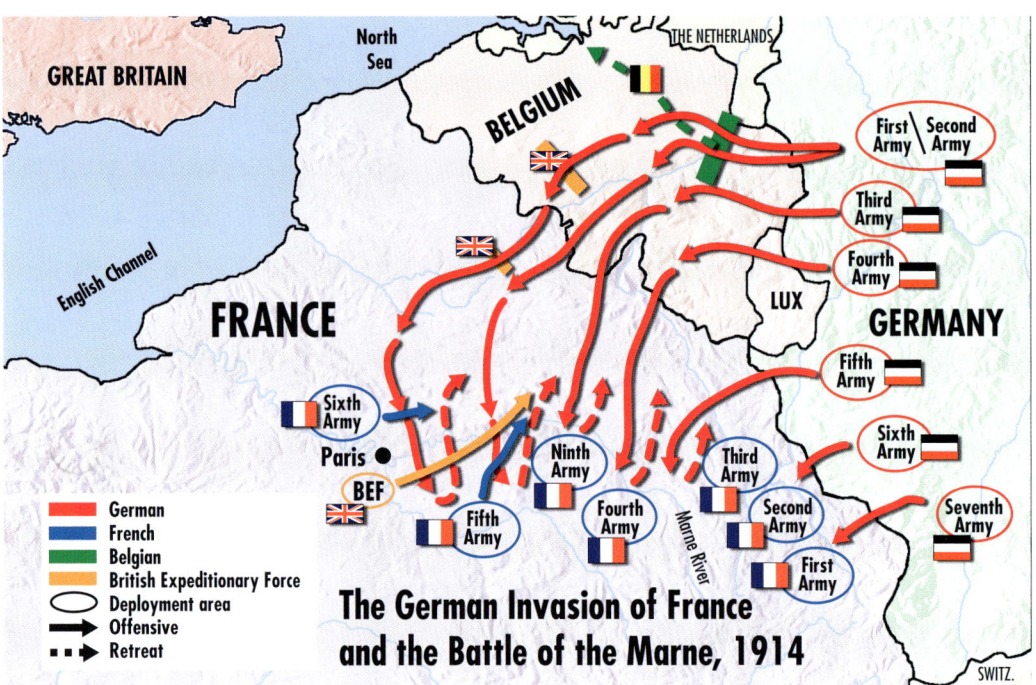

The German Invasion of France and the Battle of the Marne, 1914

By early September, the German army moved to within 30 miles (48 km) of the French capital of Paris. But there were problems. By invading Belgium, the Germans brought Great Britain into the war. Britain had a treaty with neutral Belgium. In the agreement, Britain promised to fight any nation that attacked Belgium. Germany suddenly found itself at war with a powerful new enemy.

Another problem with the Schlieffen Plan was that German supply and communication lines were dangerously thinned out. After weeks of pushing deep into France, German soldiers were exhausted, and supplies were often scarce.

German General Helmuth von Moltke modified the Schlieffen Plan. He thought his army was on the verge of conquering French forces. He ordered his army to swing to the southeast to meet the enemy. This mistake exposed the German right side, or flank. French and British forces sprang into action and attacked the vulnerable German flank.

Marshal Joseph Joffre

Joseph "Papa" Joffre (1852-1931) commanded French forces for the first 30 months of World War I. Joffre believed the French fighting spirit would overcome any foe. This "offensive to the utmost" policy caused tragic losses. He did not adapt well to new situations. Joffre was valuable, however, for his refusal to panic. It was his calm that kept French forces going during the worst of the early parts of the war. He resigned as chief of the French army in December 1916. Four months later, the popular French "Papa" traveled to the United States. American troops were desperately needed in Europe, and Joffre helped organize them.

Joseph Joffre
"We must let ourselves be killed on the spot rather than retreat."

French soldiers are transported to the Battle of the Marne via taxis and busses.

As the German army passed into the valley of the Marne River, French commander Joseph Joffre ordered a counterattack. French reserve troops were rushed to the battlefield. They used any kind of transportation available. That included more than 600 Renault taxicabs from Paris. They became known as the "taxis of the Marne."

By September 6, more than two million soldiers faced each other on the battlefield. They clashed over the next several days. Wave after wave of men rushed at each other, only to be cut to ribbons by machine gun fire. By the time the battle was over, the French lost more than 250,000 soldiers. The Germans suffered similar casualties. The British lost 12,733 men.

Despite the heavy losses, the French and British succeeded in stopping the Germans. France had been saved. The battle today is often called "The Miracle of the Marne."

However, the Germans still held a large amount of captured French territory. They retreated and gathered their forces north of the Aisne River and built protective trenches. After a failed Allied attack, the French and British also began digging trenches.

Within a few months, both sides faced each other in a line of trenches that stretched from Switzerland in the south to Belgium's North Sea coast. The two sides were at a stalemate, unable to advance around enemy defenses. This line was called the Western Front. It would be the scene of horrifying slaughter for the next four years.

The Christmas Truce of 1914

For a week during Christmas 1914, soldiers on both sides of the Western Front stopped fighting and came out of their trenches to celebrate the holiday. Church services were held, and gifts exchanged. Near Ypres, Belgium, soldiers from Germany and Britain actually played a game of soccer (the Germans won the match, 3-2). After the holiday, fighting resumed. The following Christmas, commanders ordered anyone who tried to repeat the truce to be shot.

TANNENBERG AND MASURIAN LAKES

August–September 1914

While Germany was fighting on the Western Front in France and Belgium, it also was fighting on the Eastern Front against the Russian army. Unlike the slugfest of trench warfare, the battles in the east were sweeping attacks that covered hundreds of miles of land.

At the beginning of World War I, Russia was an ally of France and Great Britain. When Germany invaded France, Russia agreed to help its allies by attacking Austria-Hungary and East Prussia, an eastern province of Germany.

Two separate Russian armies attacked. The Russian forces were huge. Most thought they could win the war easily. However, the troops were poorly trained and ill-equipped.

The commanders of the two Russian armies, Pavel Rennenkampf and Aleksandr Samsonov, hated each other. They did not communicate well. Worse, the Russians used radio transmissions that were intercepted by German forces. The messages were not coded, so the Germans knew exactly what the Russians were planning. Poor training, bad equipment, incompetent leadership, and no element of surprise would spell disaster for the Russians.

Generals Hindenburg (at the binoculars) and Ludendorff (center back) during the Battle of Tannenberg.

Russian soldiers scramble over a steep hill to attack German forces.

In August 1914, Russia's Second Army, led by Samsonov, found itself in the forest region near the village of Tannenberg, in East Prussia. The Germans were led by General Paul von Hindenburg, who was teamed with Erich Ludendorff. Together they masterminded a strategy to encircle the Russians. On August 26, the trap was sprung.

Thousands of men swept across the battlefield. The Germans had far better artillery and supplies. They destroyed the right and left flanks of the Russian army. Then they encircled the center, trapping the enemy. The Russians quickly ran out of food, ammunition, and other supplies.

Unable to continue fighting, the Russian Second Army collapsed by the end of August. Nearly 100,000 Russian soldiers were captured. About 50,000 were killed or wounded. General Samsonov, unable to face Russian leader Czar Nicholas II, committed suicide in disgrace.

Germany suffered about 20,000 killed or wounded in the battle, far fewer than the Russians. As a bonus, the Germans captured hundreds of artillery guns.

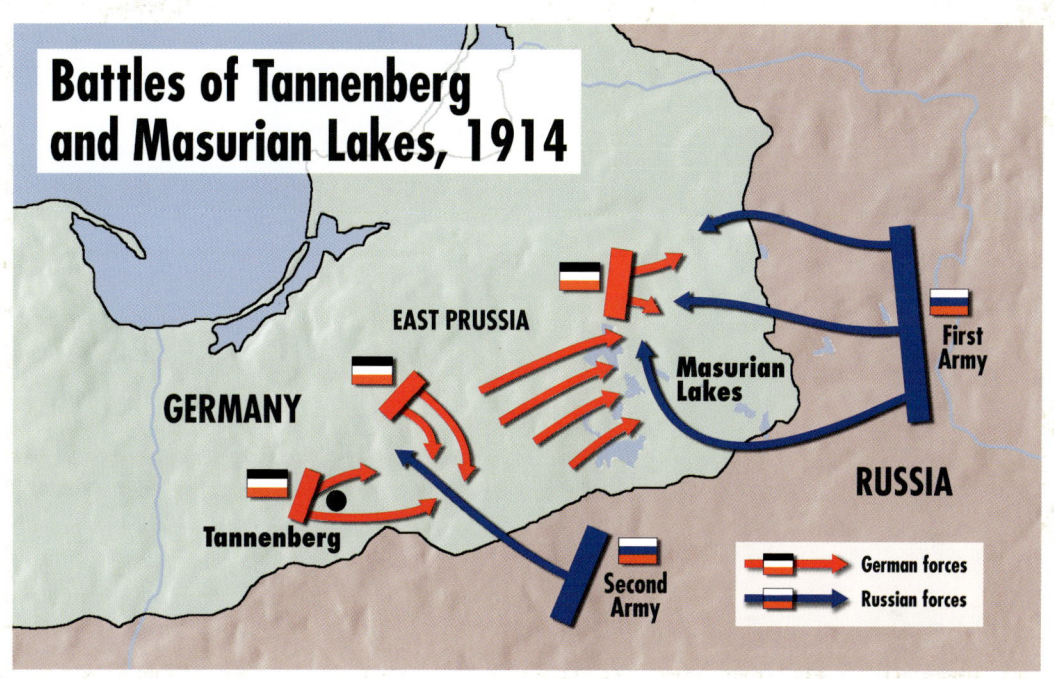

Well-armed German soldiers sweep across an open battlefield in 1914.

Ill-prepared and poorly led, Russian troops flee the battlefield.

The following September, German forces trapped General Rennenkampf's First Army at the First Battle of the Masurian Lakes, in East Prussia. Once again, the Russians found themselves enveloped by superior German forces. The Germans thrashed the Russians, who were forced to withdraw from German territory after suffering more than 100,000 casualties.

Russian forces would later have some success against Austria-Hungary, but by 1916 the Germans controlled the entire Eastern Front. Hindenburg and Ludendorff were hailed as heroes in Germany.

The defeats at Tannenberg and the Masurian Lakes completely demoralized the Russians. This led in part to the government's collapse and the Russian Revolution of 1917.

General Paul von Hindenburg

Paul von Hindenburg
"In war, only the simple succeeds."

Paul Ludwig Hans von Hindenburg (1847-1934) was born into a military family. He fought in several wars until his retirement in 1911. In 1914, he was called to service once again as commander of the Eastern Front. His victories against Russian forces made him a national hero. Together with military strategist General Erich Ludendorff, he came up with a plan to starve Great Britain into surrendering by using submarine attacks on all ships. Sinking unarmed ships eventually led to the United States joining the war, and ultimately, to Germany losing it. After the war, in 1925, he was elected president of Germany's Weimar Republic. When Hindenburg died in 1934, Adolf Hitler took control of Germany.

GALLIPOLI

February 1915–January 1916

In 1914, the Ottoman Empire (today's Turkey) joined the Central Powers of Germany and Austria-Hungary. Because of this, Russia declared war on the Ottomans.

An important waterway called the Dardanelles runs through a part of northwestern Turkey. It connects the Aegean Sea (a part of the Mediterranean Sea) to the Black Sea. Russia needed access to these vital shipping lanes. But by declaring war on Turkey, it could no longer send ships through the narrow waterway.

Great Britain wanted to help its Russian ally by capturing the land surrounding the Dardanelles. Winston Churchill, the First Lord of the Admiralty (similar to the U.S. Secretary of the Navy), was the operation's chief planner.

In April 1915, the Allies gathered troops from Britain, France, Australia, and New Zealand and loaded them onto ships. The soldiers from Australia and New Zealand were called Anzacs (Australian and New Zealand Army Corps). They were known as some of the best fighters of the war.

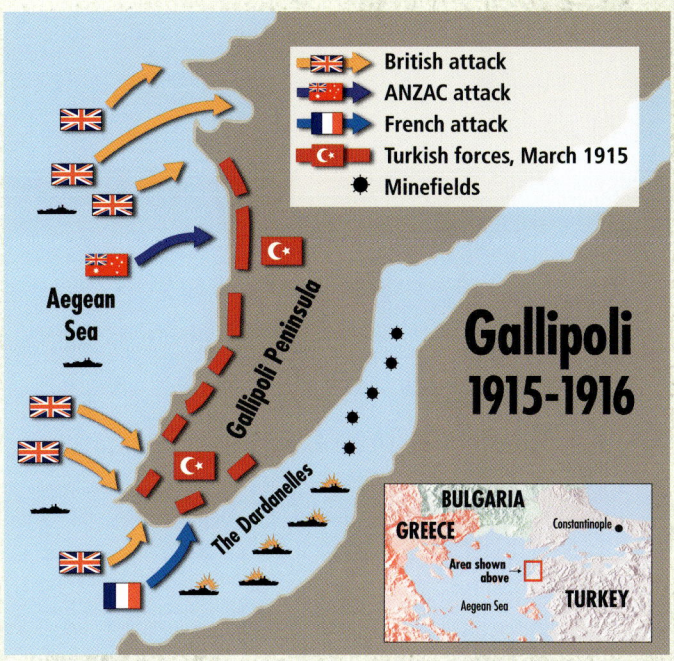

On April 25, the Allies landed at Gallipoli, a peninsula on the western shore of the Dardanelles. They hoped to eventually capture the Ottoman capital of Constantinople, but they didn't even come close. The enemy was well prepared for the invasion. The Allied troops quickly found themselves bogged down on the hot and disease-ridden coast.

After nearly a year of futile combat, the Allies finally evacuated their forces by January 1916. They suffered approximately 265,000 casualties. The Ottomans held off the invasion, but at a steep price of about 300,000 men.

Australian troops charge "over the top" during the Dardanelles Campaign in Gallipoli, 1915.

VERDUN

February 21–December 18, 1916

"The enemy started to advance in mass down the railway cutting, about 800 yards off, and Maurice Dease fired his two machine-guns into them and absolutely mowed them down. I should judge without exaggeration that he killed at least 500 in two minutes. The whole cutting was full of bodies and this cheered us all up." –Lieutenant K. Tower, Royal Fusiliers, 1914

Late in 1915, German General Erich von Falkenhayn sent a letter to Kaiser Wilhelm II. He told the emperor of a plan to help Germany break the stalemate of trench fighting on the Western Front.

Falkenhayn was convinced that Russia was on the verge of revolution, and would soon pull out of the war. Victory for Germany meant concentrating on French forces. If Germany could beat France, then Britain would also give up the fight, and the war would be won. "The strain on France," Falkenhayn wrote, "has reached the breaking point."

France's Fort Douaumont before (1915) and after (1916) the Battle of Verdun.

French soldiers in the trenches at Verdun.

To crush the French forces, Falkenhayn chose to attack a single point along the trench line. It was a place so important that the French would "throw in every man they have." If the enemy took the bait, Falkenhayn was convinced the attack "would bleed France white." This strategy was called a "war of attrition." It was used by both sides during the war. The idea was to inflict as many deaths or injuries on the enemy as possible, to the point where they either couldn't fight any longer or simply gave up.

Falkenhayn chose to attack the fortress city of Verdun. It is located in northeastern France near the border with Germany. Circling the city was a series of forts. Verdun and the forts controlled access to eastern France. The French could not afford to lose this vital piece of ground.

German infantry troops march toward the front line at Verdun, France, in 1916. The gruesome and bloody Battle of Verdun was fought from February 21, 1916, until December 18, 1916.

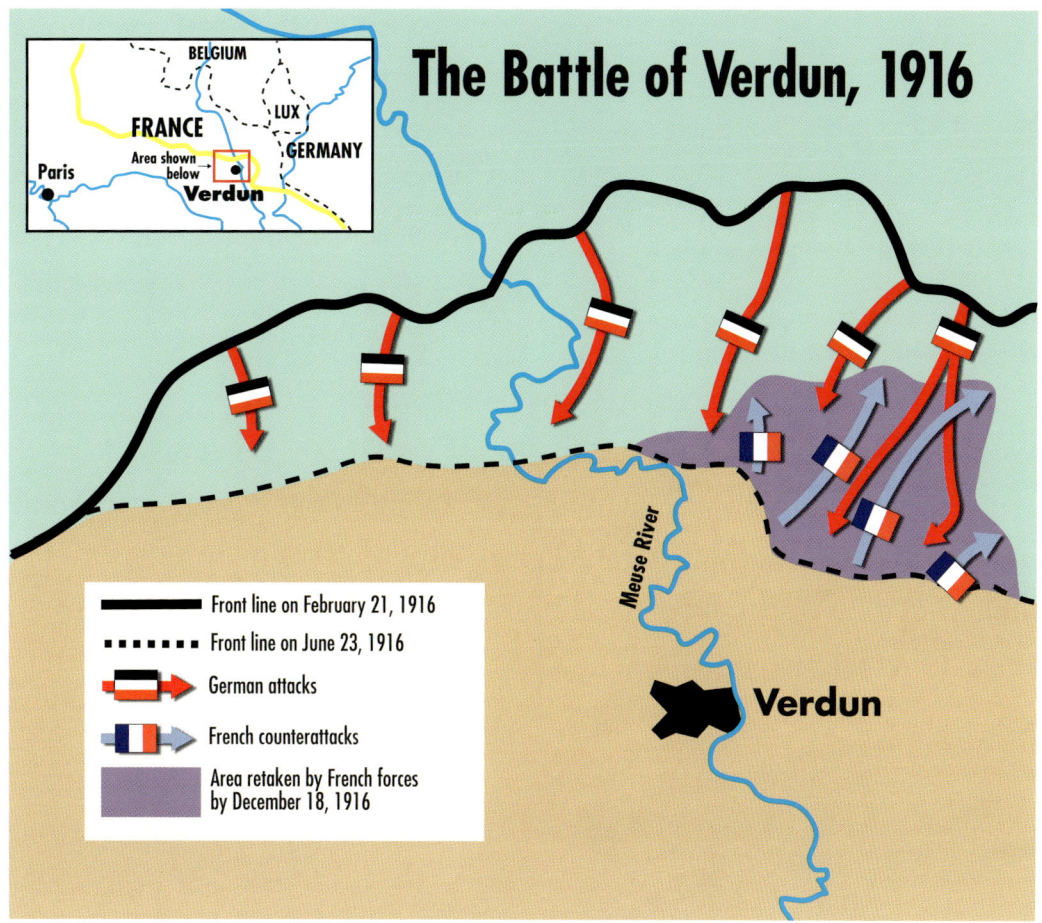

On February 21, 1916, the Germans began a massive attack. They launched constant artillery bombardments against the forts, and sent wave after wave of troops onto the battlefield. For four days the Germans advanced and captured several key forts and positions.

By February 25, French reinforcements arrived, along with a new commander, General Henri Philippe Pétain. He organized an effective defense of Verdun. He also uttered the famous rallying cry, *"Ils ne passeront pas!"* (They shall not pass!)

That summer, French resistance stiffened. Allied forces pushed the Germans back almost to the place where the attack had begun.

By July 1916, the Germans were forced to call off the main assault on Verdun because of a new Allied attack to the north that was launched by British forces. This offensive would soon become known as the Battle of the Somme.

As for Verdun, Germany almost succeeded in bleeding France white, but they also suffered great losses themselves. The slaughter was horrifying, and in the end, almost no ground was taken.

The French launched a counterattack in the autumn. They drove back the Germans and ended the threat to the city of Verdun. By December, they had retaken most of their forts, including the stronghold of Fort Douaumont.

After 10 terrible months of mindless killing, the Germans inflicted about 500,000 casualties, while suffering 430,000 killed and wounded of their own, including many of their best troops.

A Verdun battle scene created for a movie.

General Henri Philippe Pétain

Henri Philippe Pétain
"We tried to spare effort, and met disaster."

General Pétain (1856-1951) began his career as an officer in the elite French mountain troops in 1876. He specialized in defensive techniques, which ran against French military thinking at the time. At the siege of Verdun, however, Pétain was called on to help. His success there made him a national hero. He became known as the Lion of Verdun. In 1917, Pétain assumed command of all French armies.

After World War I, Pétain became a civilian politician. Early in World War II, after the defeat of the French military, he negotiated his country's surrender to the Nazis. He then helped set up an occupational government controlled by Germany. Because of this treason, the hero of Verdun went down in history as the man who betrayed his country.

THE BATTLE OF JUTLAND

May 31–June 1, 1916

Most of the fighting in World War I was on land, but some action took place on the seas. The British used many of their warships to escort merchant vessels. They also blockaded Germany, choking off supplies. The Germans used their fleet to protect their coastline from invasion.

In order to shut down supplies of food and weapons to Great Britain, the Germans used submarines, called U-boats. Over the course of the war, these silent hunters sank more than 5,000 merchant ships. However, Allied torpedoes and bombs sent 178 German submarines to the bottom of the sea.

The only major sea battle of World War I happened in the North Sea in 1916, off Denmark's Jutland Peninsula. On May 31, the German High Seas Fleet and the British Grand Fleet opened fire on each other. Even though there were more British ships, Germany had the edge in newer, better-armed vessels. The British lost 3 battlecruisers, 3 cruisers, 8 destroyers, and 6,094 sailors. The Germans lost a single battleship, 1 battlecruiser, 4 light cruisers, 5 destroyers, and 2,551 men.

The Germans inflicted more damage, but the British won the battle by keeping control of the seas. Britain's vast fleet kept the Germans bottled up in their home ports for most of the rest of the war.

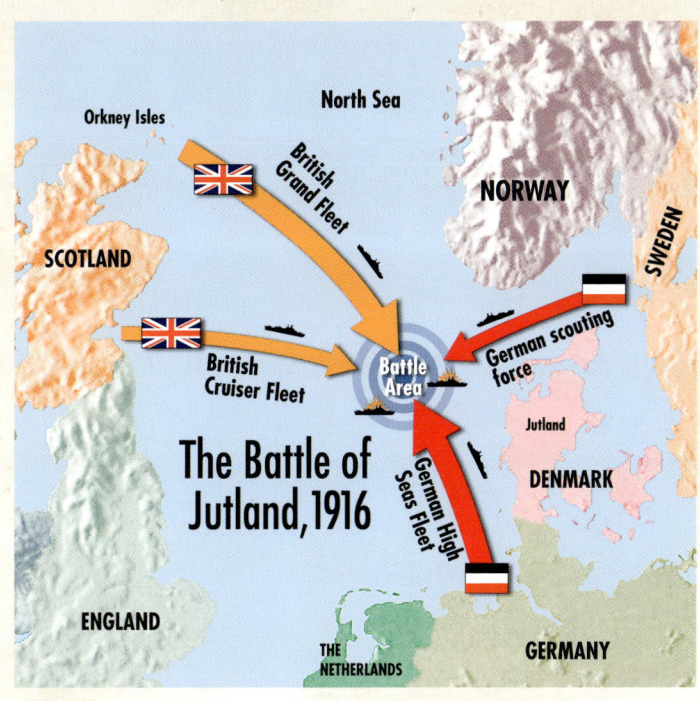

Battleships at the Battle of Jutland on May 31, 1916.

SLAUGHTER OF THE SOMME

July 1–November 18, 1916

"Yesterday I visited the battlefield…. The place was scarcely recognizable. Instead of a wilderness of ground torn up by shell, the ground was a garden of wild flowers and tall grasses. Most remarkable of all was the appearance of many thousands of white butterflies which fluttered around. It was as if the souls of the dead soldiers had come to haunt the spot where so many fell. It was eerie to see them. And the silence! It was so still that I could almost hear the beat of the butterflies' wings." —A British officer, 1919

As the Battle of Verdun raged in eastern France, British and French war planners, including British Field Marshal Sir Douglas Haig, tried to find a way to break through the German trench lines. The generals decided to launch a massive attack near the Somme River in northeastern France. They hoped to smash the German armies there. They also wanted to force Germany to pull troops away from the fortress city of Verdun. That would relieve pressure on French forces, who were barely hanging on for their lives.

British soldiers take cover behind a hill.

A French rail gun fires at German troop positions during a night attack.

The Battle of the Somme was planned to be a big push that would end the war. More than 120,000 troops from the British Expeditionary Force (BEF), along with as many men as the French could spare, were set to attack along a 25-mile (40-km) front. Instead, the battle became the scene of unbelievable carnage and senseless slaughter, some of the worst in the war.

A week before the attack, the Allies began an intense artillery barrage. They hurled more than 1.6 million shells against the Germans using 1,400 artillery guns. The plan was to destroy the enemy's trenches and artillery, plus kill or shock Germany's troops. Then, Allied infantry would march in to mop up whatever resistance remained.

However, the Germans moved underground into their deep, heavily fortified dugouts. They simply waited out the artillery attack. Although the explosions were terrifying and deafening, the artillery didn't cause significant damage to the German forces. Also, much of the barbed wire in no-man's-land remained intact.

A fortified German dugout at the Somme combat zone.

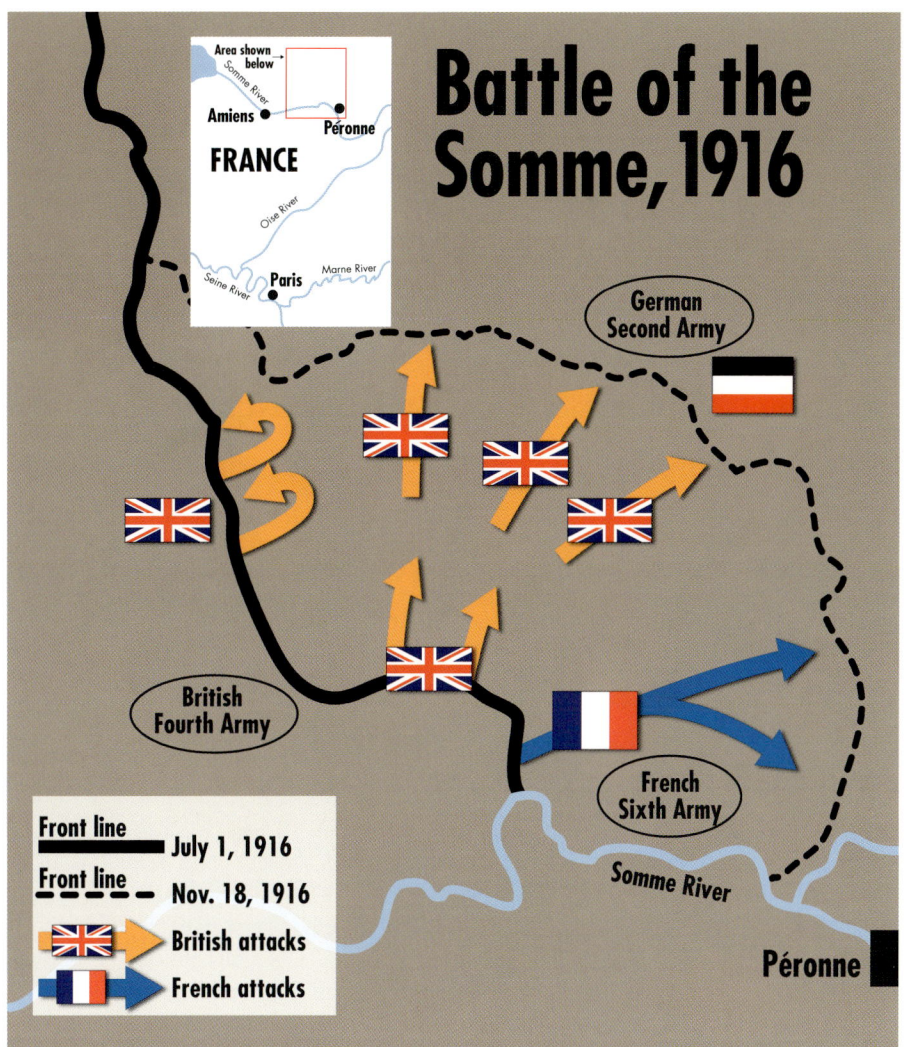

On the morning of July 1, the first British soldiers attacked. The generals were so confident that their artillery had wiped out the Germans that they ordered their troops to walk in an orderly way into the battlefield. Some units followed these orders, but most soldiers dashed across no-man's-land toward the enemy. A deadly surprise awaited them.

The Germans popped up from their bunkers. More than 100 heavy machine guns had survived the artillery bombardment. As the British troops poured from their trenches into the open, the Germans opened fire with machine guns and rifles. The British were cut to pieces. Many became tangled in barbed wire and could not escape the murderous enemy fire.

The slaughter of the first attack was shocking, even to the most battle-hardened troops. By the end of the day, the British suffered a staggering 57,000 casualties. About 20,000 of those men were killed. It was the largest single-day loss in British military history.

Despite the terrible cost, Field Marshal Haig sent wave after wave of his troops against the Germans. French forces also joined the battle. Small gains were made, but there was no great breakthrough as the Allies had hoped for. By November, the freezing rain and snow turned the battlefield into a muddy quagmire, putting an end to the bloodbath.

When the battle finally ground to a halt, the Allies gained about 10 miles (16 km) of territory, but at a cost of 430,000 British and 200,000 French casualties. The Germans suffered approximately 450,000 casualties. The Battle of the Somme became one of the bloodiest in world history.

By the following spring, the Germans had pulled back to the "Hindenburg Line," a new string of fortified trenches and bunkers farther to the east. More than one million men had fallen during the Battle of the Somme, seemingly for nothing. The stalemate on the Western Front continued.

Soldiers struggle through barbed wire as they cross no-man's-land during the bloody Battle of the Somme.

Sir Douglas Haig

Douglas Haig
"The idea that a war can be won by standing on the defensive and waiting for the enemy to attack is a dangerous fallacy."

Sir Douglas Haig (1816-1928) was a field marshal, the highest rank in the British army. Before World War I, he fought battles and commanded armies in Africa and India. He took command of the British Expeditionary Force (BEF) on the Western Front in 1915 and served through the end of the war. Many have praised Haig's leadership skills, especially during 1918, when Germany's army was pushed back toward their own border. However, many other people remember him as "Butcher Haig," the leader who needlessly sent hundreds of thousands of men to their death at the Battle of the Somme.

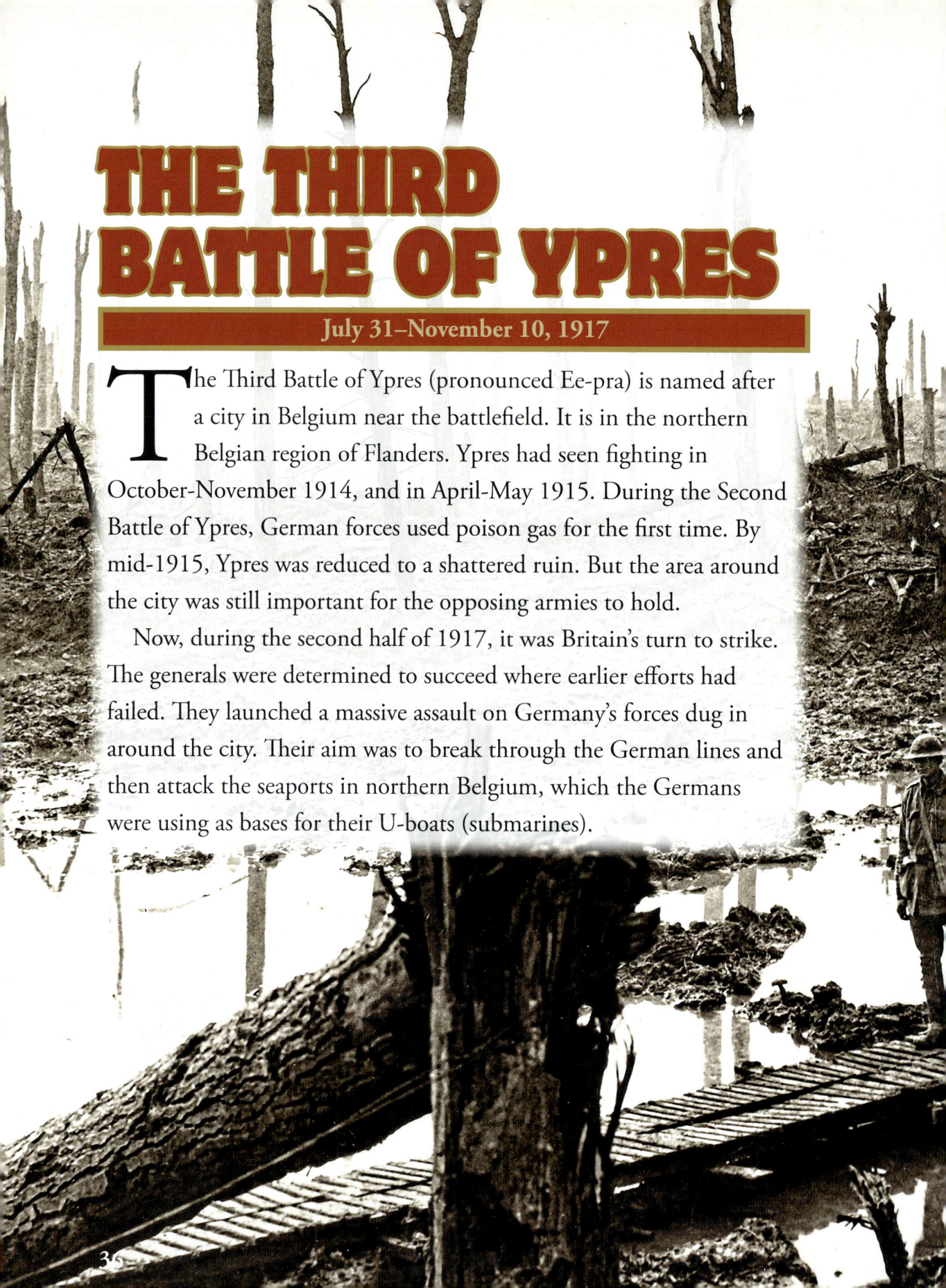

THE THIRD BATTLE OF YPRES

July 31–November 10, 1917

The Third Battle of Ypres (pronounced Ee-pra) is named after a city in Belgium near the battlefield. It is in the northern Belgian region of Flanders. Ypres had seen fighting in October-November 1914, and in April-May 1915. During the Second Battle of Ypres, German forces used poison gas for the first time. By mid-1915, Ypres was reduced to a shattered ruin. But the area around the city was still important for the opposing armies to hold.

Now, during the second half of 1917, it was Britain's turn to strike. The generals were determined to succeed where earlier efforts had failed. They launched a massive assault on Germany's forces dug in around the city. Their aim was to break through the German lines and then attack the seaports in northern Belgium, which the Germans were using as bases for their U-boats (submarines).

Australian troops walk through the bombed out remains of Chateau Wood, during the Third Battle of Ypres in Belgium.

British artillery soldiers in Belgium in 1917.

The battle started in mid-July with a massive artillery barrage, even bigger than the bombardment at the Battle of the Somme. Artillery shells rained down on German troop positions for two weeks, with more than four million shells churning the soil and stripping the landscape.

On July 31, the infantry attack began. The result was much the same as at Verdun or the Somme. Waves of men were mowed down by machine gun fire, with little to show for their sacrifice.

Adding to the horror was the mud. The drainage system on the flat plains of Flanders had taken many generations to construct. Allied shelling destroyed it in a matter of weeks. When the autumn rains came, there was nowhere for the water to go.

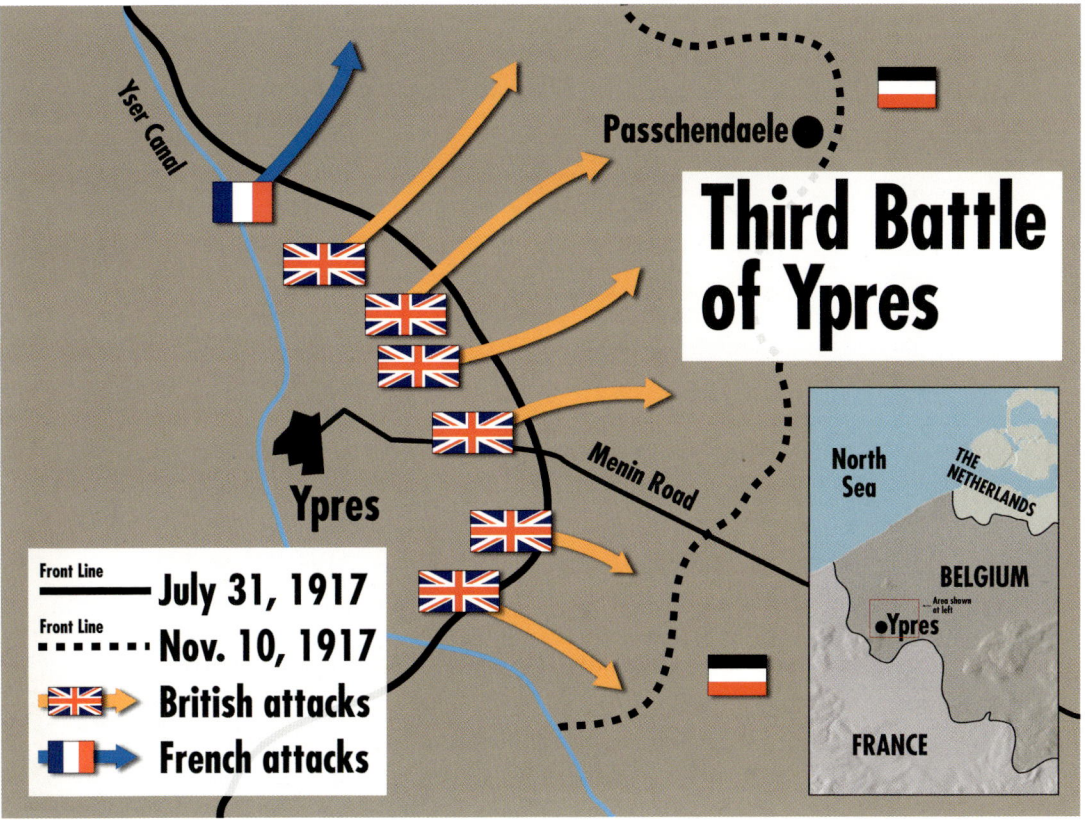

In August and October 1917, the heaviest rains in 30 years turned the shattered battlefield into a muddy quagmire. Many of the injured soldiers couldn't free themselves and literally drowned in the brown soup. A British officer wrote, "The ground is churned up to a depth of ten feet, and is the consistency of porridge." In the final stages of the battle, about one-fourth of the British dead were drowning victims.

Canadian troops captured the shattered village of Passchendaele on November 6. (The Third Battle of Ypres is often called the Battle of Passchendaele.) By November 10, the Allied forces finally halted the offensive. The Allies had gained barely 5 miles (8 km) of territory in three months, at a cost of about 253,000 Allied and 260,000 German casualties.

THE WORLD AT WAR

Most of the fighting of World War I took place in Europe. But with 36 nations taking part in combat, fighting also erupted in many other parts of the world.

In Africa, British forces captured German colonies, including Togoland (today's Togo), Cameroon, and German South West Africa (today's Namibia). But in German East Africa (comprised mostly of today's Tanzania), brilliant German Lieutenant Colonel Paul Emil von Lettow-Vorbeck and his African army kept Allied soldiers at bay until after the end of the war in November 1918.

German East Africa Askari troops march in orderly formation.

In China, Japanese and British forces attacked and seized the German-controlled port of Tsingtao in 1914. By capturing the important Chinese harbor city, the Allies denied Germany a base for its ships in the Pacific Ocean.

In Southern Europe, Italy joined the Allies in 1915 and invaded the borderlands of western Austria-Hungary. The Austro-Hungarian army became stretched thin fending off a massive Russian attack to the east (the Brusilov Offensive), and from invading Serbia to the south. With help from Germany, they won a major victory against the Italians at the Battle of Caporetto (in today's Slovenia) in 1917. The Austro-Hungarian and German forces would eventually be defeated by the Allies, but not before months of brutal warfare. Much of it was fought in the mountainous terrain of the Eastern Alps. Each side lost hundreds of thousands of men.

Austrian troops haul artillery into the Alps.

THE DESERT WAR

In 1914, the Ottoman Empire controlled a large part of the Middle East, including Palestine (today's Israel), Syria, parts of Arabia, and Mesopotamia (today's Iraq). The British, along with many troops from India, attacked Mesopotamia in November 1914. They captured the port city of Basra to make sure shipping continued from the oil-rich region. The new British fleet of battleships used engines that required oil to run.

The Sinai and Palestine Campaign began in 1915 when Ottoman forces attacked the British-held Suez Canal in Egypt. The canal was vital for ships to move between the Mediterranean Sea and the Red Sea. The attack failed.

In the following years, Britain sent thousands of soldiers to push the Ottomans out of the region. Led for most of the campaign by General Edmund Allenby, they captured important cities such as Baghdad, Jerusalem, and Damascus.

The Imperial Camel Corps Brigade near Beersheba, Palestine. The ICCB was tasked with pushing the Ottomans out of the region.

Thomas Edward Lawrence

The legendary Colonel T.E. Lawrence (1888-1935) was a British archeologist and soldier. He was sent to the Middle East and advised Emir Faisal, who was a leader in the Arab Revolt against the Ottomans. Lawrence spoke Arabic, wore traditional robes, and adopted other customs among the Arab Bedouin people. He also fought alongside them. From 1916 to 1918, they attacked railroads and forts in a successful guerrilla campaign to disrupt the enemy. Lawrence became known as "Lawrence of Arabia." After the war, Lawrence was bitterly disappointed when the major European powers secretly divided up the Middle East instead of creating an independent Arab state, as they had promised.

T.E. Lawrence
"To me an unnecessary action, or shot, or casualty, was not only waste but sin."

TIMELINE

1914

June 28: Austria-Hungary's Archduke Franz Ferdinand is assassinated by a Serbian nationalist while touring Sarajevo, the capital of Bosnia-Herzegovina.

August: World War I fighting begins as German armed forces invade Belgium and France. Most of Europe, including Great Britain and Russia, soon enters the war.

August 26-31: Russia suffers a major defeat at Battle of Tannenberg.

September 5-12: First Battle of the Marne. The German invasion into France is halted.

September 9-14: Second massive Russian defeat, this time at Battle of the Masurian Lakes.

1915

1915-1923: Turkish forces slaughter ethnic Armenians living within the Ottoman Empire. The Turkish government accuses the Armenians of helping the Russians. Casualty totals vary widely, with estimates between 800,000 and 2 million Armenians killed.

Feb 1915-Jan 1916: The Battle of Gallipoli. British forces invade the Gallipoli Peninsula along the Dardanelles, but are driven back by Ottoman forces.

April 22: Germans are first to use lethal poison gas on a large scale during the Second Battle of Ypres.

May 7: A German U-boat sinks the unarmed British passenger liner *Lusitania*, killing 1,198 people, including 128 Americans. The American public is outraged, but President Wilson manages to keep the U.S. neutral.

1916

Feb 21-Dec 18: Battle of Verdun. Nearly one million soldiers are killed or wounded.

May 31-June 1: Battle of Jutland.

1916 - Continued

June 24-Nov 18:   Battle of the Somme causes approximately 1.25 million casualties. On the first day of the infantry attack, July 1, British forces suffered a staggering 57,000 casualties, including 20,000 dead.

1917

January 31:   Germany declares unrestricted submarine warfare, outraging the American public.

March 15:   The Russian Revolution overthrows Czar Nicholas II.

April 6:   The United States declares war on Germany.

July 31-Nov 10:   Third Battle of Ypres. The Allies lose more than a quarter-million men for a mere five miles (8 km) of territory.

November: Tanks are used for the first time on a large scale at the Battle of Cambrai. And on November 7, Russia is taken over by Lenin's communist government during the Bolshevik Revolution.

December 15:   Russia's Bolshevik government agrees to a separate peace with Germany, taking Russia out of the war.

1918

Mar 21-July 17:   Germany mounts five "Ludendorff offensives" against strengthening Allied forces. The attacks are costly to both sides, but Germany fails to crush the Allied armies.

May 30-June 26:   American forces are successful against the Germans at Chateau-Thierry and Belleau Wood.

Sept 26-Nov 11:   French and American forces launch the successful Meuse-Argonne Offensive.

Sept 27-Oct 17:   British forces break through the Hindenburg Line in several places.

November 11:   Armistice Day. Fighting stops at 11:00 AM.

1919

May 7-June 28:   The Treaty of Versailles is written and signed.

GLOSSARY

Allies
Great Britain, France, and Russia formed the Allies in 1914 at the outbreak of World War I. Japan also joined the Allies, but played a minor role. Russia dropped out of the war in 1917. Italy joined the Allies in 1916, followed by the United States in 1917.

Artillery
Large guns, too heavy to carry, that fire explosive shells at the enemy from a great distance. Coordinated artillery barrages can cause massive destruction without exposing friendly ground troops to enemy fire.

Casualties
Soldiers killed or wounded in battle.

Central Powers
In World War I, the countries fighting against the Allies: Germany, Austria-Hungary, Turkey, and Bulgaria.

Diplomacy
Peaceful relations between countries, including making treaties and trade agreements. In 1914, diplomacy failed, propelling most of Europe into declaring war.

Eastern Front
Unlike the static trench warfare of the Western Front, the Eastern Front of World War I was characterized by large, sweeping maneuvers over open terrain. In the opening years of the war, Russian forces moved into Germany and Austria-Hungary, but by March, 1918, the German army penetrated deep into Russia.

Flank
In military terms, the right or left side of a formation, or force. Exposing one's flank to the enemy is very dangerous, causing confusion and heavy casualties.

No-Man's-Land
The area of land between two opposing lines of trenches.

Russian Revolution
The 1917 revolution in which Russia's ruler, Czar Nicholas II, was overthrown. The first part of the revolution occurred in February/March, when an uprising brought a government to power headed by Aleksander Kerensky. The second part is called the October Revolution (or the Bolshevik Revolution), in which Kerensky's government was overthrown by a group called the Bolsheviks, led by Vladimir Lenin, who placed Russia under a communist government. Shortly after the Bolsheviks took power, Russia withdrew from fighting in World War I. This was called a "separate peace," an agreement reached with Germany without first consulting Russia's allies.

Western Front
Established by December 1914, the Western Front was a network of trenches that stretched across eastern France and a section of western Belgium. The Western Front ran approximately 400 miles (644 km), reaching from the North Sea to the border of Switzerland.

To learn more about the battles of World War I, visit abdobooklinks.com. These links are routinely monitored and updated to provide the most current information available.

INDEX

A
Aegean Sea 20
Africa 35, 40
Aisne River 13
Allenby, Edmund 42
Allies 4, 13, 20, 21, 25, 26, 28, 32, 34, 38, 39, 40, 41
Alps, Eastern 41
America (*see* United States)
ANZAC (Australian and New Zealand Army Corps) 20
Arab Revolt 43
Arabia 42
Australia 20
Austria-Hungary 4, 14, 18, 20, 41

B
Baghdad, Mesopotamia 42
Balkan region 4
Basra, Mesopotamia 42
Belgium 9, 10, 13, 14, 36
Black Sea 20
Britain (*see* Great Britain)
British Expeditionary Force (BEF) 32, 35
Brusilov Offensive 41
Butcher Haig (*see* Haig, Douglas)

C
Cameroon, Africa 40
Caporetto, Battle of 41
Central Powers 4, 20
China 41
Christmas 1914 13
Churchill, Winston 20
Constantinople, Ottoman Empire 21

D
Damascus, Syria 42
Dardanelles 20, 21
Dease, Maurice 22
Denmark 29

E
East Prussia 14, 16, 18
Eastern Front 14, 18, 19
Egypt 42
Europe 4, 11, 40, 41

F
Faisal, Emir 43
Falkenhayn, Erich von 22, 24
First Army (Russia) 18
Flanders (region) 36, 38
Fort Douaumont 26
Fossil Monarchies, The 4
France 4, 8, 9, 10, 12, 14, 20, 22, 24, 26, 30
Frontiers, Battle of the 9

G
Gallipoli 21
German East Africa 40
German South West Africa 40
Germany 4, 8, 9, 10, 13, 14, 16, 18, 19, 20, 22, 24, 26, 27, 28, 29, 30, 32, 35, 36, 41
Grand Fleet, British 29
Great Britain 4, 10, 13, 14, 19, 20, 22, 28, 29, 36, 42

H
Haig, Douglas 30, 34, 35
High Seas Fleet, German 29
Hindenburg, Paul von 16, 18, 19
Hindenburg Line 34
Hitler, Adolf 19

I
India 35, 42
Iraq 42
Israel 42
Italy 41

J
Jerusalem, Palestine 42
Joffre, Joseph "Papa" 11, 12
Jutland Peninsula 29

L
Lawrence, Thomas Edward 43
Lawrence of Arabia (*see* Lawrence, Thomas Edward)
Lettow-Vorbeck, Paul Emil von 40
Lion of Verdun (*see* Pétain, Henri Philippe)
Ludendorff, Erich 16, 18, 19

M
Marne, First Battle of the 8, 12
Marne, The Miracle of the 12
Marne River 12
Masurian Lakes, First Battle of the 18
Mediterranean Sea 20, 42
Mesopotamia 42
Middle East 42, 43
Moltke, Helmuth von 10

N
Namibia, Africa 40
Napoleon 4
Nazis 27
New Zealand 20
Nicholas II 16
no-man's-land 32, 33
North Sea 13, 29

O
Ottoman Empire 4, 20, 21, 42, 43

P
Pacific Ocean 41
Palestine 42
Paris, France 10, 12
Passchendaele, Belgium 39
Passchendaele, Battle of 39
Pétain, Henri Philippe 25, 27

R
Red Sea 42
Renault taxicab 12
Rennenkampf, Pavel 14, 18
Royal Fusiliers 22
Russia 4, 8, 14, 16, 20, 22
Russian Revolution 7, 18

S
Samsonov, Aleksandr 14, 16
Schlieffen, Alfred von 8
Schlieffen Plan 8, 10
Second Army (Russia) 16
Serbia 41
Sinai and Palestine Campaign 42
Slovenia 41
Somme, Battle of the 26, 32, 34, 35, 38
Somme River 30, 38
Suez Canal 42
Switzerland 13
Syria 42

T
Tannenberg, Battle of 18
Tannenberg, East Prussia 16
Tanzania, Africa 40
Taylor, Edmond 4
Togo, Africa 40
Togoland, Africa 40
Tower, Lieutenant K. 22
Tsingtao, China 41
Turkey 4, 20

U
U-boats 28, 36
United States 4, 7, 11, 19, 20

V
Verdun, Battle of 30, 38
Verdun, France 24, 25, 26, 27, 30, 38

W
Weimar Republic 19
Western Front 13, 14, 22, 34, 35
Wilhelm II 8, 22
World War II 4, 27

Y
Ypres, Belgium 13, 36
Ypres, Second Battle of 36
Ypres, Third Battle of 36, 39